Playmakers

Shortstops

Lynn M. Stone

Rourke
Publishing LLC
Vero Beach, Florida 32964

www.rourkepublishing.com

PHOTO CREDITS: All photos © Lynn M. Stone

Editor: Robert Stengard-Olliges

Cover and page design by Tara Raymo

Library of Congress Cataloging-in-Publication Data

Stone, Lynn M.
  Shortstops / Lynn Stone.
     p. cm. -- (Playmakers)
  ISBN 978-1-60044-597-2
  1. Shortstop (Baseball)--Juvenile literature. I. Title.
  GV870.5.S76 2008
  796.357'24--dc22
                                         2007019510

Printed in the USA

CG/CG

Rourke Publishing

www.rourkepublishing.com – rourke@rourkepublishing.com
Post Office Box 3328, Vero Beach, FL 32964

Table of Contents

The Shortstop   4

The Shortstop's Skills   10

So, You Want to Be a Shortstop? 18

Glossary   23

Index   24

The Shortstop

The shortstop is one of the four **infielders** who plays behind the pitcher and catcher on a baseball **diamond**. A shortstop usually lines up between second and third base. In special situations, a shortstop may play much closer to second base or even in **shallow** center field.

The shortstop (far left) crouches at his position as the pitcher throws toward the plate.

If you're thinking about being a shortstop, you had better be right-handed. A right-hander can easily throw to first or second base. A lefty would lose valuable time by having to turn his body for the throw.

Shortstops throw right-handed although they may be left-handed batters.

A shortstop scoops up a hard-hit ground ball and straightens up to throw to first base.

The shortstop position is perhaps the most challenging of all the infield positions. A shortstop must be able to quickly move left or right to field **struck balls**. A shortstop needs a strong arm since he has a longer throw to first base than a second baseman. A shortstop tends to have more fielding chances because most baseball players swing right-handed. Right-handed hitters generally **pull** baseballs; that is, they hit the ball to the left side of the field toward the shortstop.

Making the play, a shortstop dashes to his right to stop a ground ball from reaching left field.

The Shortstop's Skills

A shortstop is typically one of the smallest players on a team. But a good shortstop is an extremely athletic and **nimble** fielder. In addition, he must possess a "good arm"— the ability to make long, strong, and accurate throws.

A young shortstop crouches to stop a hard-hit ball.

Nimble and quick, a shortstop watches a ground ball until it is safely in his glove.

Part of the shortstop's athleticism is on display when he charges a **ground ball**, or when he quickly bolts to his right or left to stop a ground ball from leaving the infield.

A shortstop makes a relay throw from the edge of the outfield back to the infield.

A good shortstop can "gobble up" ground balls with ease and routinely throw the ball to first base before a runner can reach safely. In some situations the shortstop may have a short throw to third base or second base. He may also have to receive a throw at second base, especially when his team attempts a **double play**.

A shortstop takes a throw at second base and throws to first to make a double play.

A common double play situation occurs when the batting team has a runner on first base and no more than one out. If the batter hits a ground ball to the first or second baseman, that fielder may attempt to throw out the runner who was on first as he dashes for second base. The shortstop's job is to cover second base to receive the fielder's throw, then fire the ball back to the first baseman before the batter reaches first base. At the same time, the runner heading to second tries to disrupt the play by sliding into second base. The best shortstops can avoid the sliding runner and still throw the ball accurately to first base!

A shortstop awaits a throw that is too late to catch a runner speeding into second base.

A shortstop covers second base between pitches to keep a base runner from running to third.

The shortstop also has to cover second base in a potential double play or force play situation when a ground ball is hit to the catcher or pitcher. The shortstop sometimes covers second base when a runner attempts to steal. In some situations, when a batter is likely to **bunt** the ball toward the third baseman, the shortstop is required to cover third base.

A typical shortstop often gives a team extra speed on the base paths.

A shortstop rushes to shallow left field to take a relay throw from the center fielder.

On long hits into left or center field, the shortstop becomes a cutoff man. As a cutoff man, he rushes into the outfield to take a relay throw from the outfielder. The shortstop then makes a snap decision about where to throw the ball next—usually third base or home plate.

So, You Want to Be a Shortstop?

The shortstop is such a busy infielder that fielding skills are a must. Throughout baseball history, many shortstops were dismissed as "good field, no hit." Even now, an exceptionally talented defensive shortstop is not expected to be one of the team's best hitters. But good hitting shortstops are far from unusual.

The shortstop's bat is important for a team's offense.

A left-handed, hitting shortstop fouls off a pitch.

A shortstop is typically one of the fastest players on a team. If he is a reasonably good hitter with a good eye, he may wind up batting high in the order, often at Number 1 (leadoff) or Number 2. The leadoff batter's job is to reach base, a job best accomplished by good hitting or by taking a **base on balls**. Light hitting shortstops typically bat low in the order.

Because shortstops are typically slender, they are not usually power hitters. There have certainly been exceptions, like former Chicago Cub Ernie Banks and one-time shortstop Alex Rodriguez of the New York Yankees.

A shortstop takes batting instruction from his Little League coach.

Glossary

base on balls (BAYSS ON BAWLZ) — the automatic awarding of first base to a batter after four pitches called by the umpire outside the strike zone

bunt (BUHNT)— a ball that a batter intentionally hits very lightly by letting the pitch strike his bat rather than swinging at the pitch

diamond (DYE muhnd) — the infield of a baseball field with its four-sided, diamond shape

double play (DUH buhl PLAY) — a play in baseball in which two outs are recorded on one pitch

ground ball (GROUND BAWL) — a ball that a batter hits on the ground

infielder (in FEEL dur) — the position of players in the infield behind the pitcher: first baseman, second baseman, shortstop, and third baseman

nimble (NIM buhl) — referring to the ability to move about quickly and with great coordination and ease

pull (PUL) — to hit a pitched baseball toward the left side of the diamond in the case of a right-handed batter and to the right side in the case of a left-handed batter

shallow (SHAL oh) — the part of the outfield closest to the infield

struck balls (STRUHK BAWLS) — pitches that are hit by batters

Index

athleticism   11

Banks, Ernie   22

base   4, 6, 7, 8, 13, 14,
    15, 16, 17, 21

challenging   8

double play   13, 14, 16

plate   5, 17

position   5, 8

relay throw   12, 17

Rodriguez, Alex   22

steal   16

throw   5, 6, 7, 8, 10, 12,
    13,14,15,17

Further Reading

Kappes, Serena. *Sports Heroes and Legends: Derek Jeter*. Lerner, 2004.
Rappoport, Ken. *Super Sports Star Derek Jeter*. Enslow Publishers, 2004.
Ripken, Cal, Jr. *Play Baseball the Ripken Way*. Random House, 2005.

Website to Visit

http://www.everything2.com/index.pl?node=shortstop
http://baseball.azplayers.com/baseball-positions.html
http://www.cocobaseball.org/generalstructure.html

About the Author

Lynn M. Stone is the author of more than 400 children's books. He is a talented natural history photographer as well. Lynn, a former teacher, travels worldwide to photograph wildlife in its natural habitat.